Don't Strike Out: Lessons for a Winning Life in Retirement

Ryan Ledden

with Dan Cuprill

Introduction

I have been a coach at heart for most of my adult life. I can't seem to get away from the game of baseball that I have loved for so long, no matter how hard I try (hence, the baseball themed title of this book). My journey has taken me through many different paths in life, all helping to inform the words on this page.

As a kid, I remember being fascinated by money... how it functions, moves, stores, creates, etc. I was too young to know the mind-blowing concept of compound interest, but that would soon come when I was 19 years old (more on that in a bit). I remember thinking about the value of saving money when my mom gave me a few pennies of change when we were at a McDonald's when I was five years old. I had no concept of what three cents could buy, but I remember thinking how much money I could save if I kept the money I was given and did not spend it. I was hooked on saving money right away.

Fast forward about 14 years when I was fortunate enough to be drafted out of high school by the Tampa Bay Rays (shout out to Mark McKnight for believing in me). I received a few pennies to sign a professional contract (more than the few I got from my mom in McDonald's). I could now go after my dream and save a few dollars for my piggy bank. Let me say that I got a decent signing bonus, and MLB would pay for my college if I were to get my degree, but it was not life-changing money like some of these players earn now. It was, however, enough to make a difference in my life long-term, so of course I wanted to save it like I did with my three cents when I was five years old.

I now had the chunk of money that I never thought I would have in my teenage years. I wanted to be responsible with that money, too. Thank God I had wonderful parents to guide me along the way. I felt like I was a responsible kid and wanted to save the money, but part of me wanted to spend it, too. My dad turned me on to "his guy" (a.k.a. a financial advisor) who worked with a lot of executives at the company he worked for at the time. I'm sure this advisor did a great job working with these executives, but I would be 'small potatoes' for him. This advisor invested my money for me but to this day, I have no idea what it was invested in. At first, there were incredible returns; my money was exploding because this was the mid- to late nineties. Anything you invested in (especially the US market) went up several years in a row...usually double digits. Then you know what happened with the start of the early 2000s and the dot com bubble.

I don't bring that brief history lesson to light to relive any painful memories for any of you. Most of your remember 2008 as your pain point. I bring all that up to share my story of education and coaching. I felt like I had:

- no idea what I was invested in
- no understanding how markets worked and
- no idea what diversification was.

That ignited my passion to learn as much as I could by reading books like this one. Let me say that the advisor who handled my money did nothing wrong. The education just was not there, but I'm thankful he didn't coach me along because this is a central part of my story and why I do what I do now.

Unfortunately, my professional baseball career only lasted for six years. I wish I could tell you I made millions and millions of dollars playing baseball, but life is not always a fairy tale. Once my career was over, I made a promise to my late mother that I would go to college if my baseball career didn't work out like I had planned. I enrolled at the greatest institution in the country, the University of Georgia. I know some of you are laughing you tails off or rolling your eyes. However, some of you are reading this with a big smile on your face in agreement, saying, "Go Dawgs!!" I graduated in three years (at the age of 27), but I still had a lot of baseball in my blood, so I wanted to be involved somehow with the game I love. That is why I became a high school teacher and a coach.

I quickly had a passion for my kids in the classroom and on the baseball field. I was fortunate to be able to teach Economics. I wanted to pass on my passion and my story to these teenagers who were about to go to college and would need to handle money for the first time for some of them. I would teach them as much personal finance as I could. Word got around to the staff that I was teaching personal finance to my students, so several teachers started emailing me or coming by my room, asking for financial advice. The more I was educating my co-workers, the more my mental wheels started turning... "Why don't I do this for a living?"

Fast forward a couple more years when my career composed of teaching and coaching was not the best fit anymore for my family for a variety of reasons. I needed to make a change. This career transition came while I had a small child and a working wife (who is the best veterinarian and mommy on the planet, I might add).

The financial services industry is a very tough industry in which one might try to 'make it.' There are many levels of success in this industry, but most don't last longer than a couple of years. I left a very safe career of teaching with a consistent income and a pension, if you stay long enough. Then to change careers to an industry in which I didn't know where my next paycheck was coming from when I first started was stressful. It can be a lucrative job, but I think many who are not in the industry think that all advisors are 'rolling in' the money. Some are, but some struggle to make ends meet.

My first two jobs in the industry were very different experiences. I'm thankful for both opportunities because they offered learning experiences, though they were not a good fit for me.   My first job was in the insurance side of the industry. Great company and great people, but selling different types of insurance was not for me. My second job was pretty much on my own as an independent advisor with a mentor that I met with every few weeks. It was a great experience, and I had a wonderful mentor, but I had a bigger vision for my career, so I moved on.

God has a funny way of putting people in our lives at the right time. I crossed paths with a gentleman in a parking lot who had been in the industry for several years at that point. He was not hiring at that time, but it sparked conversation the led to him offering me a job about a year later. Fast forward to four years later, and now I am the owner of that financial planning firm.

We are a firm that comprises true financial planners, and we walk alongside people as their lives change and evolve. We want to make a difference in our clients' lives, and we do that by coaching and educating them, which goes back to why I initially entered this industry (I don't mean for that to sound like a sales pitch, but it kind of does. However, it is true.)

Now that you know a little about me and what makes me tick, here's a little more information about this book. Our firm has conducted retirement planning seminars for people who are sick of work and ready to make a major change in their life. It can be a rather stressful time, for mistakes made at this stage cannot be reversed.

This book is a personal finance book like no other: it contains very few numbers. Lord knows we have plenty of books that do, and we're not smart enough to improve on them. This book is also rather short for two reasons. One, I don't want you to fall asleep if you haven't already; and two, the message is a simple one: the future is not predictable, unless you have a time traveling DeLorean.

We will describe many of the quantitative aspects of personal finance, but the biggest obstacle to investor success remains the investor himself. We are human, and as humans, we are naturally wired to eschew pain. We seek pleasure when we can, but the absence of pain is paramount.

It is this "survival mechanism" that kept early cave dwellers motivated to stay warm, find food, and avoid sabretooth tigers. Today, it keeps us fat, avoiding exercise (which for many is painful), and eating fast food (which is pleasurable), while contracting diabetes and hypertension along the way.

The survival mechanism has also caused the average investor, according to the DALBAR Quantitative Analysis of Investor Behavior, to buy high (because winners bring pleasure) and sell low (so we can avoid even more pain), resulting in sub-par rates of return. What worked for caveman can spell destruction in the consumer-happy world we live in now.

When entering the investing world, we accept the premise that returns will not be consistent; but we forget it as soon as we suffer a down month, or God forbid, a down year. Rather than logically accept that returns, like life, are never linear, we panic, convincing ourselves that this time the Zombie Apocalypse is real. Then we sell. Then we realize the error of our ways and start investing again...after the market has recovered.

A second major threat that requires rescue is taxation. Unlike past generations, Baby Boomers and beyond must deal with the intricacies of having their retirement savings in accounts like 401k's, 403b's, and IRA's. Most, if not all, of these accounts have never been taxed. The piper is paid at retirement. What if taxes rise in the future to finance our ever-increasing national debt?

Other threats facing today's and tomorrow's retiree include Social Security (when do I take it? how will it be taxed?) and long-term healthcare. So is the individual investor simply doomed to fail? Not at all. Steps can be taken to put the odds for success in your favor, but you must first understand what you may not know.

Lastly, we wish to extend our appreciation to Dan Cuprill for contributing sections from his own book, Retirement Rescue.

Lesson Number One: There is No Nostradamus

"Uncertainty is the only certainty there is and knowing how to live with insecurity is the only security." --John Allen Paulos

Imagine a TV network dedicated to fortune telling. Every day, it features highly educated people who strongly believe they can predict the future. Like Isaiah, they offer their prophecy for free. Unlike Isaiah, these seers are wrong about 80% of the time.   Yet, despite the failures, viewers continue to watch. Even worse, many stake their entire personal fortunes on the advice.

Would you watch such a network? Millions do. In fact, there isn't just one such channel, but two: Fox Business Channel and CNBC.

Go ahead...turn them on, especially around noon on a weekday. These channels bring on one market "expert" after another to give out stock tips or some insight as to where the market is headed.

Here's a little reality: No one...and we mean no one...knows where investment markets are headed in the next week, month, or year. If they did know, they certainly wouldn't tell you for free. In fact, they wouldn't tell you at all because such information would be far too valuable to even sell.

Remember the rule of transitive properties from math class (more on her in a minute). If A is greater than B...and B is greater than C, then A is also greater than C. Or to put it another way, if Bill is taller than Mike, and Mike is taller than Jim, then Bill is also taller than Jim. Got it?

Okay...now pay very close attention.

Markets react to news. Do you agree? Every time stocks drop in price, isn't there always some news event attributed to it?   Recall 9/11, Microsoft anti-trust suit, the Fed raising interest rates, earnings reports lower than expected?

News is unpredictable. Do you agree? Did you know any of the following events would happen before they actually occurred?

1. Hijacked airplanes crashing into the World Trade Center and the Pentagon.
2. The Kennedy Assassination.
3. The announcement of Toxic Asset Relief Program.
4. Arthur Anderson's false accounting of Enron.
5. Pearl Harbor (okay...this one isn't fair. You probably weren't alive).

In response to each of these news events, equity markets dropped rapidly. If you did know about these events a week before they actually occurred, you could have made billions of dollars.

Two movies come to mind that demonstrate this reality.

Casino Royale (2006): James Bond seeks to defeat a card playing terrorist who makes huge rates of return by shorting stocks on companies and then staging acts of sabotage on those corporations because he knows it will drive down their stock price. In other words, he knows the news before anyone else because he's creating it.

Wall Street (1987): Gordon Gekko hires aspiring trader Bud Fox to "stop sending me information and start bringing me some." So, Bud breaks into offices at night, spies on company executives, and relays insider information told to him by his father. As a result, Gekko has "news" that no one else has, allowing him to trade ahead of the market.

So, if news is unpredictable and market performance reacts to news, then market performance is unpredictable.

Wait a minute. Are you saying then that all those Wall Street experts like Jim Cramer and Charles Paine really have no idea what they're talking about?

Yes...and no. They certainly know many things. But so do millions of other traders. Everything they know is already factored into a stock's price. It's what they don't know, the future news, which will drive stock prices. They are simply speculating as to what they think the news will be.

Sometimes they get it right...most of the time they get it wrong. Studies show that on average 80% of all professional portfolio managers fail to beat their benchmark index. Of the 20% who do, very few repeaters exist.

The Law of Large Numbers

Imagine we fill the Paul Brown Stadium with 35,000 people. On the PA system, we instruct them all to stand up and remove a quarter from their pocket.

On our mark, they all flip the coin. Those who flipped heads (about 17,500) remain standing. Those who flipped tails sit down. We now repeat this exercise, again and again. With 35,000 people flipping coins, we are willing to bet our houses that at least one person in the stadium will flip heads ten straight times. In fact, we wouldn't be surprised if at least 20 people did it.

The law of large numbers states that if you have enough people try to do something, then someone will succeed regardless of skill level. The individual who tossed heads 10 straight times...is he an expert coin flipper? Does he somehow understand the gravitational properties between his quarter, his wrist, and the earth? Or was he just lucky?

Guess how many professional portfolio managers exist today? Yup...about 35,000. Over 2,000 work for Fidelity alone. Someone is bound to speculate correctly on the market's reaction to news that has yet to occur.

The successful coin flipper is called lucky. The successful stock picker is called a guru and gets his face on magazines.

Again, we'll concede that these people are smart. Most went to the very best business schools in the country where they were taught that markets and stock prices are not predictable. But when they arrived on Wall Street, they were told how their firms really make money: trades.

Over 1 billion trades a month at $9 per trade on the New York Stock Exchange alone. You do the math. It is in *their* best interest to trade...not yours.

We do think that these very smart people honestly believe they have found a peek into the future. If there were only a handful of them researching companies, then they might actually be onto something. But there exist thousands, all crunching the same data. Furthermore, their efforts to buy and sell ahead of the market incur costs that lower their rates of return.

In 2013, Eugene Fama won the Nobel Prize in economics for stating in the 1960's that something is worth only what someone is willing to pay for it. Called The Efficient Market Hypothesis, Fama showed (with a bunch of math) that the current price of a stock or bond is the correct price. Nothing is overvalued or undervalued until someone offers or agrees to a different price.

If you buy a house for $300,000, spend $50,000 for improvement, and put it up for sale, how much is it worth if the highest offer you receive is $290,000?

Correct. It's worth $290,000.

So if it's true for real estate, why not stocks?

The $6 watch

Zach Norris is a young man with a passion for fine watches. Understanding that people often don't know the value of their old jewelry, he routinely visits thrift shops and garage sales looking for great deals. If he sees a watch that he knows he can quickly resell for a profit, he will buy it for the asking price and then quickly find a new buyer. In January of 2015, he bought a $6 watch at his local Goodwill store and then sold it for $35,000.

Norris is to watches what Wall Street portfolio managers aspire to be to stocks. But unlike Mr. Norris, they deal in public information. Had Goodwill known the watch was worth $35,000, would they have sold it for $6? Or, would the prior owner have given away the watch to Goodwill in the first place? Of course not. Mr. Norris had insider knowledge. In this case, he can legally act on it. But in the world of security trading, such a move can land you in jail (see Martha Stewart and Bud Fox).

Perhaps there was a time when news traveled slowly enough for someone to get a jump. Those days are over.

There is no Nostradamus. News occurs randomly, and so too will stock and bond prices. All we have going for us is that, over the history of mankind, good news has outperformed bad. Despite world wars, famines, epidemics, assassinations, national debt, and disco, capitalism finds a way to improve the quality of life. The quality of your life today dwarfs that of every king and queen of the middle ages. It dwarfs that of your great grandparents, and even your grandparents. Is it not only logical to assume that in the future, we will witness massive amounts of bad news, but we will prosper despite it?

We don't need Nostradamus to conclude that leaning on optimism is the realistic way to view the future. Hence, actions like market timing and stock picking are far less likely to succeed than buying, holding, and rebalancing a broadly diversified portfolio.

Don't Just Take Our Word for It:

The Investment Answer by Daniel Goldie and Gordon Murray

Random Walk Down Wall Street by Burton Malkeil

The Smartest Investment Book You'll Ever Own by Dan Solin

What Wall Street Doesn't Want You to Know by Larry Swedroe

Winning the Loser's Game by Charles Ellis

Lesson Number Two: Yes, You Will Use This Someday.

"Mathematics are well and good, but nature keeps dragging us around by the nose. "

–Albert Einstein

You remember your high school math teacher. That matronly woman who has been teaching out of the same book for thirty years because "the math hasn't changed." As you looked at the inside cover of the book, you saw the names and years of the prior holders. "Was it as boring for Fred Saddlemire in 1968 as it is for me now?" you asked yourself.

The one question that rose above all others was, "Will I ever need to know this stuff?"

She assured us we would. Now you're about to see she was right.

Meet Hans & Franz. When not pumping iron and injecting themselves with steroids, they are drawing income from their savings accumulated from years on late night TV. Aside from an occasional State Farm commercial, the two are pretty much retired.

Convinced that no one should invest like a girlie man, Hans has invested heavily in equities under the belief that over time, he stands to earn a higher rate of return. Chances are he'll be right.

Franz is no stranger to machismo, but opts for a portfolio that is likely to produce a lower, but more consistent rate of return. Starting with one million each, they both desire to withdraw $50,000 per year to supplement their SNL royalty checks.

Hans and Franz are about to learn what Mrs. Cheeseman taught us years ago.

Average return may not be as important as consistency of return.

Hans: $1,000,000			
Year	Withdrawal	Return	Y/E Value
1	$50,000.00	-13	$826,500.00
2	$50,000.00	-20%	$661,200.00
3	$50,000.00	5%	$694,260.00
4	$50,000.00	-7%	$599,161.80
5	$50,000.00	20%	$658,994.16
6	$50,000.00	25%	$761,242.70
7	$50,000.00	-25%	$533,432.03
8	$50,000.00	45%	$700,976.44
9	$50,000.00	30%	$846,269.37
10	$50,000.00	20%	**_$908,060.56_**
Return Average: 8%			

Franz: $1,000,000			
Year	Withdrawal	Return	Y/E Value
1	$50,000.00	6%	$1,007,000.00
2	$50,000.00	8%	$1,087,560.00
3	$50,000.00	7%	$1,163,689.20
4	$50,000.00	11%	$1,236,195.01
5	$50,000.00	-4%	$1,138,747.21
6	$50,000.00	6%	$1,154,072.04
7	$50,000.00	12%	$1,236,560.69
8	$50,000.00	-2%	$1,162,829.48
9	$50,000.00	10%	$1,224,112.42
10	$50,000.00	6%	**_$1,244,559.17_**
Return Average: 6%			

As you can see, although Hans indeed earned a higher average return (8% vs. 6%) at the end of ten years, he has considerably less money than his body-building brother. Why? Every year, the two sell a part of their portfolios' shares to generate cash. When shares rise in value, it requires fewer shares to generate $50,000. When share prices fall, we must sell more. Those extra shares, once sold, are gone. It matters not what a portfolio does in the future in relation to those shares. They will never return.

By minimizing his potential downside, Franz has more money even though he averaged less over time. Fewer negative years means he sells fewer shares.

This phenomenon exists only because Hans and Franz need to sell shares for cash. Had they never needed to take money, then Hans would have much more money than Franz, despite the volatility. This is the Math of Retirement.

High school statistics taught us that nothing in life performs consistently--not the weather, not your golf score, and certainly not an investment portfolio. This lack of consistency can be measured. It is called standard deviation. The lower the standard deviation, the more likely you will earn the average return each and every year. So, if you find a portfolio with a guaranteed return of 8% every year, then the standard deviation is zero. Good luck finding that. Chances are, the best you'll do in seeking your 8% is a portfolio with a standard deviation of ten. So, what does that mean?

If Average Return is 8% and Standard Deviation is ten, then:

66% of the time: You will have a one-year return between -2% and 18%.

95% of the time: You will have a one-year return between -12% and 28%.

99% of the time: You will have a one-year return between -22% and 38%.

If you are an investor, then your portfolio also has a long-term average return and a standard deviation to go along with it. The problem is that very few people know this, nor do they understand the "normal" volatility that comes with it. If they did, we think they'd be much less likely to panic.

For example, if a portfolio has the dimensions described in the chart above, should we be surprised (or even disappointed) if we earn a return of -6% in a given year?

Of course not. We already know going in that this is very likely. We also know that over time, it's more likely that we'll have more positive results than negative results. Guaranteed? No. Likely? Yes.

Think of it like baking a cake. You can put in the best ingredients, but you have liquid unless you put the batter in the oven for the right amount of time.

Results do not come in a linear fashion, no matter how badly we wish they did. What in life does? Do the giant redwoods of northern California grow the same number of feet every year? Does it take you the same number of minutes to drive to work each day? Do farmers dig up their corn seeds every few days to see if they are sprouting, or have they learned to trust the process?

It is essential that you know the long-term average return and standard deviation of your portfolio allocation. Without knowing, you are simply winging it; and your survival mechanism stands a much better chance of overriding your logic.

Know your math. Make your high school math teacher proud as well as your Economics teacher!

Don't Just Take Our Word for It:

The Intelligent Asset Allocator by William Bernstein

All About Asset Allocation by Richard Feri

Asset Allocation by Roger Gibson

Lesson Number Three: The Boogeyman is Real

"The only two things that scare me are God and the IRS" –Dr. Dre

Assuming that you do not define patriotism by the amount you pay in taxes, what follows should be useful.

If you're one of the 53% of Americans who pay federal income taxes, then it is likely you pay more than what is legally required. If you own a small business, then it's almost a certainty you are over paying.

The Seven Most Expensive Words in the English Language: My CPA takes care of my taxes.

From our experience, most CPAs do a great job of filing taxes; but very few actually do any real tax planning. I ask people when the last time their CPA said he found a way to lower their taxes by $4,000, and they usually give me a blank stare and say, "Never."

Does your CPA/Tax Preparer ever:

- Call you with proactive strategies to achieve a tax-free retirement?

- Demonstrate how to restructure your 401k/403b/IRA accounts to avoid future taxation?

- Advise how to collect your social security benefits TAX FREE?

- Show you how to structure your business to minimize employment taxes?

- Show you how to write off your family's medical bills as a business expense?

- Show you how you can hire children (or grandchildren) to shift income from yourself to them?

- Help you choose the right retirement plan for your business?

- Explain how each of your investments is taxed and make suggestions on how to reduce them?

- Advise you on how to carefully consider which investments belong in taxable accounts and which investments belong in tax-advantaged accounts?

- Develop a plan for maximizing the value of any long-term capital loss carryforwards?

- Explain the rules governing "passive" income and losses and have a plan to avoid "suspended" losses?

- Meet with you throughout the year to discuss your business--or does he just wait until taxes are due?

- Give you a plan for minimizing taxes-- or does he/she just wing it every year?

Aside from investing behavior, income taxes are the greatest obstacle to most investors. There is never an age at which you stop paying them. You paid tax on your social security as you put money into the system, and you will likely pay tax on the money as it comes out.

When you reach age 70.5, you must start paying tax on your retirement plans (401k, IRA, 403b). When you die, your heirs must also pay tax on whatever is left.

Your estate may be taxed again for simply being too big.

The code is, by design, very complicated. Too often, people just go along with it, unaware of the steps that can legally reduce their federal and state income taxes. This is especially important during retirement.

You have a choice of paying taxes now...or later. To many, procrastination seems logical when it comes paying the IRS. For years people have socked away massive amounts of money in 401ks, 403bs, IRAs. The idea is you invest it now in a tax deductible/tax deferred account while you're in a high tax bracket. Then you withdraw it at a lower tax bracket when you retire. Or so you hope.

What if taxes rise in the future? Our country, as of 2017, owes close to $20 trillion (By the time you read this it will probably be over $20 trillion). Projections suggest this amount will continue to rise as more and more baby boomers retire. Fewer people will be paying taxes and more will be requiring things like Medicare, Medicaid, and Social Security. Since income taxes begin in the early 1900's, the average top marginal rate is 62%. Today it's 39.6%. We've had much higher taxes in the past.

We should be prepared for them in the future.

Case Study

Bill and Karen Tucker are both 65. Retired, Bill has a rollover IRA worth $600,000. Bill collects $2,200 a month from social security. Karen receives $1,800.

They need $7,000 a month to live comfortably, so they withdraw $3,000 a month from their retirement accounts.

To determine how much of their social security check is subject to taxation, we add the IRA withdrawals ($36,000) to one-half of the social security payments ($24,000)

This gives them a modified adjusted gross income (MAGI) of $60,000. Whenever the MAGI exceeds $44,000 for a married couple, then up to 85% of their check is subjected to taxation.

Assuming they file jointly and use the standard deduction, Bill and Karen owe about $4,000 in Federal income taxes. Within that amount is a tax assessed to almost half of their Social Security benefits.

Now, what if they had decided a few years back to convert their rollover IRAs to a Roth IRA? Doing so would have triggered tax at the time of conversion, but no tax would ever be owed on the accounts again. Even if their accounts double in value, there is no tax associated with a Roth withdrawal. Not only is there no tax on Roth IRA withdrawals, but now there would also be no tax owed on their Social Security benefits. Furthermore, Bill and Karen could still withdraw about $23,000 from their taxable IRA and still pay $0 in tax since they still have their standard deduction and exemption to apply against these "taxable" earnings.

Imagine if federal income tax rates double in the future. By converting to a Roth, the Tucker's have protected themselves.

Another tax advantaged/tax free vehicle is permanent life insurance. Money in the policy grows tax deferred and can be accessed tax free via a policy loan or withdrawal. While we don't recommend all retirees buy life insurance, it can be a fit for some depending on what they are trying to accomplish. Tax free access to your money via a policy loan or withdrawal can be a great reason to keep your policy even after you've stopped working. Plus, we are all going to die, so the death benefit is an added bonus for those love ones we leave behind. In addition, many new policies today allow you to apply a portion of the death benefit toward long term care costs. Again, not a recommendation for everyone, but could be worth exploring for some.

Like a lot of people we meet, the Tuckers rely solely on their accountant for tax advice. But from our experience, many accountants work as tax filers, not tax planners.

Tax planning is one of the most ignored areas of financial planning, and failure to address the IRS lien on savings is ruining people. It is not the job of the IRS to tell you how to lower your taxes. It's your job. If you don't know how, you need to find a professional who does. You won't find him inside a box of turbo tax software.

The tax code is very complicated. Too often people just go along with it, unaware of the steps that can legally reduce their federal and state income taxes. Failure to address this issue can mean you're not worth anywhere close to what you may think.

If you want to know more about real tax planning, call us at <u>770-382-5792.</u> We'll show you how we use our **Retirement Scorecard** to grade retirement plans for our clients. You can also attend one of our upcoming workshops and/or webinars by visiting www.completegameretirement.com.

Don't Just Take Our Word for It:

<u>How to Pay Zero Taxes 2016</u> by J.K. Lasser

<u>The Power of Zero</u> by David McKnight

<u>Look Before You LIRP</u> by David McKnight

Lesson Number Four: It will probably end badly

"It's paradoxical, that the idea of living a long life appeals to everyone, but the idea of getting old doesn't appeal to anyone." –
Andy Rooney

The first chapter ended with a statement that the future is always likely to be better than the past. For society as a whole, we truly believe that. As for our individual lives, however, we know that life is finite. The Grim Reaper is undefeated. And while modern medicine has made huge strides in fighting heart disease, diabetes, and cancer, we all still die.

The lucky ones will die suddenly, like Tim Russert. Here today living life to the fullest...gone tomorrow. Sad for our loved ones, but much better than dying a slow death where our health declines daily, limited to a wheelchair, incapable of recalling our children's names, and needing assistance to visit the bathroom.

Depressing...isn't it? That's life.

As a society, we are living longer. That is a good thing, but that also means our money must last longer. It means that eventually we will become weak and likely to need help with those things we only want to do for ourselves (custodial care).

Some stats from the National Institute for Health:

- If you reach age 65, there's a 70% chance you'll need custodial care.
- The average nursing home stay is almost three years.
- The average nursing home cost is $70,000 a year.
- Nursing home costs rise at twice the average inflation rate.
- Medicare doesn't pay for Long Term Care.

- Medicaid is available only after you've spent down your assets.
- Most people in nursing homes are on Medicaid, but they didn't start there.

Basically, you have three options when it comes to long term care.

- First, you can self-insure the exposure. Perhaps you have enough money to do just that. Remember...it's $70,000 a year now. At 6% inflation, the price will double in twelve years. If you're married and you get sick, will that leave enough money for your healthy spouse?

- Second, you can rely on Medicaid. Why not? Most do, but, that's available only after you've spent down your own money. If you're married, Medicaid kicks in when you have about $100,000 left. You don't have to sell your house, but the government may attach a lien to it after you die so that it can recoup the cost of your care.

- Third, you can buy long term care insurance. For many people, this is the right choice. Often we hear people say they won't buy it out of fear they'll never use it, and thus waste their money. We're going to let you in on a little secret: the people who go to nursing homes with long term care don't win the game. It's those who have long term care insurance but die peacefully in their sleep, healthy today...dead tomorrow, who win the game.

When your car isn't stolen, do you regret owing auto insurance? Never feel regret for being prudent.

Long term care insurance can be expensive, but a few things can be done to reduce it:

1. Limit coverage to four years. Odds are very high you won't need the policy after four years (you'll die). By limiting coverage to four years, you reduce the cost dramatically over a lifetime benefit policy.
2. Self-insure a part of the cost. If nursing homes in your area cost $200 per day, consider coverage for $150. Be sure to study the long-term impact of not being fully insured.
3. Ask your children to pay for it. They are the ones who stand to benefit from you not spending all their inheritance on nursing home care.

Whatever you do...have a plan! It's not a matter of if, but when!

Don't Just Take Our Word for It:

Long Term Care: <u>Your Financial Planning Guide</u> by Phyllis Shelton

Lesson Number Five: Your Brain is Messed Up

"We have seen the enemy, and he is us."—Pogo

Perhaps the biggest obstacle (no, not *perhaps*...it really *is* the biggest) preventing financial success is our own brain...our humanness...our emotions.

God gave us many gifts, but if misused, they can be self-destructive.

Consider weight loss. Technically, losing weight is very easy. We simply exercise more and eat less. Yet we are the fattest nation on earth, and weight loss is a multi-billion-dollar industry.

Investing is also quite simple: buy when prices are low. Sell when they are high. According to the Dalbar study, we see that simple strategy ignored all the time. People often do the complete opposite.

Let's take Marty McFly's time traveling Delorean back a few years....to 10,000 BC.

Meet your great, great, great, great, great, great, great, great, great (you get the idea) grandfather. We'll call him Fred. He lives in a cave with his mate Wilma and their children, Pebbles and Bam Bam (who they adopted after a T-Rex ate Barney & Betty Rubble).

Life is very simple for Fred and Wilma. Fred wakes up, sharpens his spear and kills whatever he can find. He brings it back to the cave where Wilma cooks it.

Fred is motivated to stop the pains of hunger, cold and predators. He seeks warmth and comfort where he can, but above all else, he tries to avoid pain for his family and himself. He doesn't know it, but Fred has within his brain a survival mechanism that motivates him to behave this way. It is his natural tendency to flee from danger. In fact, all animals have it--

another gift from God. Fred doesn't worry about his cholesterol level, his A1C results, or his blood pressure. He merely wants to stay fed, warm and safe. Fred was the original couch potato whenever the opportunity presented itself.

Food, water, safety and warmth...that's all he thinks about. Morality, personal fulfillment, spirituality...these don't matter to him at all. It's a struggle just to meet the basics.

Fast forward to present day. We don't have Fred's worries. Far from it. Food? In the U.S., a major health problem amongst our poor is obesity. Water, warmth...readily available. But the survival mechanism that kept Fred alive until a sabre-toothed tiger ate him is still present in our brains. We don't use it often, but it's there...lurking.

Need to lose weight by eating less (painful) and exercising (even more painful)? Forget it. Our brain tells us we're crazy. Stay in bed. Rest. Relax.

Fred didn't care if he lived past age 40, but you do. Rather than helping you though, the survival mechanism is betraying you.

When your stocks fall in value, you experience pain. Your brain tells you that you must do something. You must sell. When what you sold starts increasing in value, you feel worse! You know logically that stocks are likely to rebound, but your brain convinces you that "this time is different."

While the survival mechanism is the worse feature of our psyche when it comes to investing, there are a few others that can be equally destructive:

Herding: When we were teenagers, we called it "peer pressure." Our mothers asked, "If Johnny told you to jump off a bridge, would you?" Hey, bridge jumping can be great fun.

When Frank in accounting tells you that everyone is dumping the index fund in the company 401k and loading up heavily on company stock, you need to remind yourself of something. Unless Frank is having secret meetings with the company chairman, he knows nothing more than the rest of the world. All the information about your company is already factored into its stock. Frank is just speculating. Sadly, there were several "Franks" working at Enron.

Confirmation Bias: We'd all like to believe that we are objective thinkers, weighing all facts before making a decision or establishing a belief. Sorry...not true. There are things we WANT to believe are true. So much so, we'll ignore any evidence to the contrary. Take Nikki's daughter, Georgie. At age 8, she is committed to believing in Santa Claus. She's heard from classmates that St. Nick isn't real, but every year she finds evidence to the contrary (thanks to her mom). In her mind, the kids who don't believe are simply the ones who misbehave and receive nothing on December 25th.

For other people, we see confirmation bias in areas like climate change, the Kennedy assassination or the future price of gold.

In 2001, Dan met a GE engineer who said he had no intention of ever diversifying away from his company stock. "I don't want to hear it," he said to us when we suggested a broader allocation. He was 64, and the stock comprised 100% of his portfolio. In the previous ten years, his net worth had tripled. It seemed invincible.

At that point, the stock was trading at $65 a share. Seven years later, it was worth $8.

When it comes to matters of finance, confirmation bias can be expensive.

Gambler's Fallacy: The roulette wheel has come up red the last six times. It must turn up black this time, right? No wait...six times in a row? It has to turn up red a seventh time. It's on a roll.

Of course, both statements are false. The gambler believes that despite randomness, past events influence future events. Therefore, casinos give free hotel rooms to high rollers. Just don't leave our casino. We know eventually you will give the money back. You believe you have skill, but we know it is pure chance...and the odds of chance favor the house.

We see it with stocks all the time. The market is up, and "experts" call for a "correction." In order for there to be a correction, we must first have a mistake. The "correction assumption" is that stocks are mispriced.   Eventually the market will wake up this reality, causing prices to adjust.

It's hogwash. News drives stock prices. Markets will move randomly because news occurs randomly.

Anchoring: Back to our GE engineer. His wife saw the potential mistake of holding just one stock, but even she couldn't be swayed toward logic because they knew diversification would trigger taxation. So anchored was she in her belief that taxes are bad, she put herself in a position of eventually owing no tax because they lost most of their portfolio in 2008. Oh, to have Marty's Delorean.

A successful investor understands that logic doesn't come naturally. He seeks out ways to ensure that when it comes to money, the left side of his brain (where logic resides) stays in control.

Don't Just Take Our Word for It:

Predictably Irrational by Dan Ariely

The Behavior Gap by Carl Richards

Lesson Number Six: Rick Perry was right.

"The real sin with Social Security is that it's a long-term rip-off and a short-term scam."—Tony Snow

---

A Ponzi scheme is an investment fraud that involves the payment of purported returns to existing investors from funds contributed by new investors. Ponzi scheme organizers often solicit new investors by promising to invest funds in opportunities claimed to generate high returns with little or no risk. In many Ponzi schemes, the fraudsters focus on attracting new money to make promised payments to earlier-stage investors to create the false appearance that investors are profiting from a legitimate business.

With little or no legitimate earnings, Ponzi schemes require a consistent flow of money from new investors to continue. Ponzi schemes tend to collapse when it becomes difficult to recruit new investors or when a large number of investors ask to cash out.

--United States Securities & Exchange Commission

In the 2012 election primary, pundits attacked Texas Governor Rick Perry for correctly describing the Social Security system as a Ponzi scheme. The system, which began in 1935, then taxed 42 workers for every retiree a maximum total of $30 per year. Today, it taxes three workers for every retiree 6.2% of their earnings (up to $118,550). If you're self-employed, you pay the tax twice.

Money is taken from workers and is transferred to retirees. The rate of return is not guaranteed. Most people will average between two and four percent. Many will lose money if they die before they receive benefits equal to their contributions. Unlike your savings, you cannot leave your social security benefits to your children. At least Charles Ponzi gave some investors a high rate of return.

Social Security today is not what it was intended to be when President Roosevelt signed the program into existence. Its original intent was to aid Americans who couldn't take care of themselves, such as widows and orphans. It was never designed to be the sole means for retirement income, which it has become for many Americans today.

In 1935, life expectancy was 62, while the earliest one could collect benefits back then was age 65. On average, you were more likely to die than receive benefits. Ironically, the very first person to receive a check, Ida May Fuller, lived to be 100 years old. These days about 58 million people receive benefits.

Benefit Timing

For many retirees, the question of when to take benefits can be a difficult one. The longer you wait to start collecting, the larger your monthly check. Full retirement age is between 65 and 67 depending on what year you were born.

You can take benefits as early as 62, but receive 25% less per month than if you hold out until your full retirement age. If you wait until age 70 to collect, then you get an extra 8% for every year you wait. In real dollars that means if your full retirement benefit is $2,000 but you elected to take it at 62, you will receive $1,500 each month. Likewise, if you wait until age 70, you will receive $2,700 every month.

Life expectancy plays a major role in determining the timing of your social security benefits. The breakeven point for taking benefits at 62 vs. 70 is age 78.

If you had that time machine and knew your expiration date – no problem. Of course, if you delay taking your benefit, it may mean you have to spend more of your savings in the early years of retirement.

Many factors need to be taken into consideration when tapping social security.

So what is the future of Social Security? Is it sustainable? What was once a 1% tax is now 6.2%. As fewer people pay in and more are recipients, the percentage could always be increased. The amount of income subject to the tax could be increased, and inflationary increases could be eliminated or decreased. Lots of appealing options...NOT.

No political party wants to broach the elimination of Social Security, and they likely won't. Social Security in its current state isn't at all what Roosevelt had in mind in 1935, so change is always a strong possibility.

Don't Just Take Our Word for It:

Get What's Yours: The Secrets to Maxing Out Your Social Security by Laurence J. Kotlikoff, Phillip Moeller and Paul Solman

Number Seven: A Pension...What's that?? There May Be Other Options.

"When I was young, many people worked for a company with a pension plan that covered them for as long as they lived. If they didn't have a pension plan, they could count on Social Security and Medicare."—

Robert Kiyosaki, author of *Rich Dad Poor Dad* — the #1 personal finance book of all time, and an entrepreneur, educator and investor

Robert WAS correct, but pensions are a dying breed and Social Security and Medicare are not enough to live on now with our consumer driven lifestyles and rising health care costs, among other things. I'm not going to go into a detailed history of pension plans, so unless you have been living under a rock for the past few decades, you know what has happened over time. Only 19% of workers have access to a pension, and most of them are government employees. There are still some private sector pension plans out there if you work for a company for 30 plus years. Private and public-sector pension plans have been giving employees many options on how they want their pension paid to them or if they would like to elect a lump sum payout.

This decision should not be made lightly, because it can have a lasting impact on your retirement, as well as your spouse and even your children. We have already talked about there being no Nostradamus, but employees need to account for every variable in their lives to make the best decision for them. There is no blanket advice here. Everyone's situation is different depending on what they are trying to accomplish. I hate to sound like an accountant (sorry to all you CPA's out there), but it all depends on numerous variables.

"Best" Pension Payout

Got you. You were looking for what I thought was the 'best' option for you. I'll be honest...I have no idea. Most people these days are looking for the 'best' and 'easiest' decision they can make based on what an expert will tell them, relying on a few bits of information. Like I said, everyone's situation is different. You must weigh every option and how the pension works best for you. [There are pros and cons to each when you are choosing a pension option or lump sum.] There are even more decisions to make once you decide to take the pension or lump sum. Let's weigh some of those options to give you a little nudge in the right direction.

Pros & Cons of Your Pension

When you take your pension as a monthly annuity (yep, you heard me right...I said annuity), you are assuring your family that you will never run out of money. Your lifestyle may need to change, but your pension will provide you an income forever (as long as the pension doesn't go under.) In theory, if you keep fogging up a mirror, you will continue to receive a check. Your spouse will continue to receive your check as well if he/she lives longer than you, but you would need to select the joint-and-survivor pension that we will discuss below. Sounds great, right?

One possible downside to a monthly annuity/check will usually be loss of purchasing power over the years because most private sector pensions are not adjusted for inflation. If they are adjusted for inflation, they usually don't keep up with inflation rates each year. Usually cost of living adjustments (COLAs) in pensions are the first option to be reduced or eliminated for their pension recipients because it saves a ton of money for the pension fund. Many public-sector pensions still have the strongest cost of living adjustments built in them. For example, I work with many retired educators in Georgia, and they have a 3% inflation adjustment each year (1.5% every six months...at least for now). However, this cost of living adjustment was 4% on an annual basis a few years ago, so you see my point concerning the stress on pensions.

Of course, as you receive your monthly pension, you will need to pay ordinary income tax on that money. You will also need to bear the risk if your employer fails to pay the benefits that it has promised you when you made your choice at retirement. On the flipside of that disaster, the federal Pension Benefit Guaranty Corporation (in many instances) will step in and take over the pension obligations. PBGC guarantees that pension recipients will receive the benefits they have earned up to a certain point. (To check current limits, you can go to their website and search for maximum monthly guarantee tables.)

Pension Options

Pensions offer a wide variety of choices, but they usually fall under one of several categories:

- Single life pension (annuity) will provide you with the largest monthly payout during <u>your</u> lifetime. It is the highest payout because the pension is only covering one life. This may be a very poor choice if your spouse will need an income once you are gone, but I don't know how much you like your spouse. If your spouse has a pension as well or has plenty of assets to cover expenses, then this still could be an option. Again, everyone's situation is different, and you must weigh the pros and cons of this option.

- Joint-and-survivor pension sends you a check for the rest of your life as well as your spouse if you pass away before he/she does. You might have the option to choose a 100%, 75%, or 50% joint-and-survivor pension. This means if you take the 100% pension option, then your spouse will receive the exact same check you received while you were alive for the rest of his/her life. A 75% pension option will pay your spouse three-quarters of your old benefits, and 50% provides half. The 100% option will pay the lowest amount to you and your spouse because it is based on covering two people instead of one. Pensions are based on actuarial numbers, so if you choose the 50% option, then it will be the highest of the joint-and-survivor payouts. There are many different factors involved with this joint-and-survivor option that must be taken into consideration. Going back to my example of working with many educators in Georgia, they have an option called a 'pop-up.' This means if you select the joint-and-survivor option and your spouse (who didn't work in the education system) precedes you in death while receiving your pension, then your payout will 'pop-up' to the full single life option which is the highest payout.

- Period-certain is an option some pension plans have that will pay your beneficiary (usually your spouse) for a set number of years after you pass way. The period-certain payout range is usually limited to five to 20 years during which your monthly check will be determined by how long of a time period you select after your death. The longer period-certain you select, the smaller the payout is to you while you are alive. This period-certain option is great for those who are single, but may want to take care of someone else they select.

Lump Sum Options

There is usually the option to take a lump sum when you retire instead of taking the pension. This is done by taking a lump sum and directly sending it to an Individual Retirement Account (IRA) that you need to have set up ahead of time, so the funds have a place to go to, so you are not taxed on one giant lump sum of money. By sending that lump sum to an IRA, you control your taxes by how much you pay yourself each month.

One of the pros of this lump sum option is a large stash of cash that you have in your name, and you have the ability to take out more from your IRA if you need it in an emergency. This could also be a negative for some people who can't control their spending. Another benefit of a lump sum option to an IRA is that your beneficiaries will inherit the amount of money that is left in your IRA at your passing. With some pension options like we just discussed, the pension stops with one person or two, but usually stops payouts beyond that. If the lump sum is large enough and managed well, it can be passed on to several generations. Depending on how your IRA is invested, this is your best option to keep up with or surpass inflation pressures you may have, depending on your pension options. However, you do run the risk of completely running out of money, because you could spend too much money, or the stock market could completely implode, and you would lose everything (if this happens, then your pension would run dry as well.)

Shouldering the entire risk of your money in an IRA is the biggest con to taking a lump sum amount. Some people do not have the risk tolerance or knowledge to put that kind of responsibility in their own hands. Rates of return are great to growing your nest egg, but lifestyle spending may have the greatest impact on your money. We discussed earlier the sequence of returns while you are spending down your nest egg in retirement. You want to get a more consistent rate of return as you are drawing your money down in retirement as opposed to chasing returns and bragging to your buddies that you got a 12% rate of return. That's great but you may have a much smaller nest egg than the guy getting a 8% rate of turn that is less volatile as they are taking an income.

Other "Pension" Options

We have already discussed Social Security options and benefits, so I am not going to explore any details here. However, Social Security income is another form of pension or annuity. There is the cuss word again, "annuity." More on annuities in just a moment. Going back to the quote at the beginning of this chapter...I don't know about you, but I don't want to think of Social Security and Medicare as a pension that I will rely on to do the things I want in retirement. Please don't misunderstand my last comment. I think Social Security planning is one of the most under analyzed decisions people make in retirement. It could mean the difference in hundreds of thousands of dollars, and many start taking a Social Security check because "they want to get a check before it runs out." This is not a good reason to start collecting this check from the federal government.

Everyone's situation is different and must be thoroughly investigated before deciding. Social Security income is an awesome way to pay your fixed expenses each month and delaying your payments will only go further in retirement especially when the government graciously gives you a cost of living adjustment (don't expect too many of these) and if you do get one, it probably won't be for much. You can go to the Social Security website and look up the tables. Retirees got a COLA of .3% in 2017 and got 0.0% in 2016. Some of the highest COLAs were back in the early 1980's when it was as high as 14.3%...those days are over my friends.

Another way to give yourself a paycheck each month is an annuity. That word gets thrown around a lot in my industry. It may be one of the most discussed, argued, and sold strategies in the financial industry. Just like every other strategy in planning, annuities have pros and cons. If you ask an annuity-only salesman, annuities are the greatest thing ever. I'm sure some of you reading this book have been to a dinner seminar and heard, "you can get a great rate of return with no downside risk." I'm sure they had a chart available to show you, too. However, money managers who navigate the stock market will tell you that annuities are the worst strategy ever. Stock pickers will tell you they can get you higher rates of return on your money; annuities are expensive; and you can't get your money out when you need it. Like I said before, there is not a good or bad strategy with your retirement planning. The strategy implemented should be what's a good fit for you and depends on what you are trying to accomplish.

Annuities get a bad rap sometimes, because they are the least understood strategy out there, and most annuity-only salesmen love to sell them because of the commissions. I'm not saying annuities are bad, but people using this strategy need to understand it and have a true teacher and coach to walk them through it. Also, I'm not against the guys using an annuity as part of an overall strategy and receiving a commission. I have been on the receiving end of an annuity commission, so I am not complaining, but it was the right fit for the client.

There are several types of annuities out there that I'm not going to pursue in detail in this book. There are several advantages and disadvantages to purchasing an annuity. The two main categories of annuities are fixed and variable annuities. There are investment options inside the variable annuity as well as different income options, death benefits, and payouts.

Variable annuities have a higher potential rate of return, but usually have higher fees inside the contract. High fees do NOT make them bad if you know what you are purchasing. Fixed annuities (and fixed index annuities) usually have guarantees built into the contract, and some companies give up-front bonuses when money is placed in a contract. The interest credited to these contracts is usually less than a variable annuity in an up market, but they have guarantees built in that lock your money when the market is down.

Annuities have different taxation depending on how you purchase them. You can purchase an annuity with after-tax dollars with which your money grows tax deferred, but you pay taxes on the growth as you take it out in retirement. You can also purchase an annuity inside your IRA and pay taxes on all the distributions (income) from the annuity/IRA.

There are several options to give your family consistent income in retirement. Each situation needs to be analyzed for the pros and cons to make the best decision for your financial future.

Don't Just Take Our Word for It:

How to Not Get Ripped Off when Buying an Annuity by Alessandra Derniat

The Truth About Buying Annuities by Steve Weisman

Protecting Your Pension for Dummies by Robert D. Gary

Number Eight: Flat Abs, a low A1C, and Wealth: To get these, you probably need help

"Everyone needs a coach. It doesn't matter whether you're a basketball player, a tennis player, a gymnast or a bridge player." --Bill Gates

On our own, we rarely perform at our optimal level. A good coach will not only help you achieve excellence, he'll assist in keeping you there. A good coach sees things we can't (or don't want to see). He forces us to leave our comfort zone and to apply logic when emotion is in overdrive. He holds us accountable to ourselves.

One of the biggest failings in the financial services industry is the inability to understand this. The industry is dominated not by coaches (or even advisors) but by commissioned salesmen. They push product as the answer and then go looking for the question. Objectivity is lost, and the client pays the price.

A good wealth **coach** services his client with a holistic approach and commits himself to putting the needs of the client first. This is what we like to call the Black Oak Wealth Coaching Program.

Step One: Consultation-- We begin every first meeting with a simple question: "What will make this a great meeting for you today?"

We want the client to set the agenda. More importantly, we want to know what keeps them up at night.

If on a scale of one to ten (ten means you sleep like Bill Gates, and one means you don't sleep at all), how do you rate your financial situation? If you are a nine or a ten, you're done. Give this book to a friend and go live your life. No need for any coaching. You are Tiger Woods in 2000.

But if you are more like a seven (or lower), then what must occur for you to be a ten, aside from winning the lottery? We find that it's rarely about the amount of money one has. The most anxious people we've ever met had significant wealth. Despite that, they were fearful, frustrated and even angry. In some cases, they were victimized by other advisors. To get most people to a ten, it takes a strategy that they have a hand in designing. They require a plan that details fully the pros and cons and is simple enough that they can explain it to a friend.

Do you need to be a financial expert to be a ten? No. Just like we don't need to know how a hybrid engine works to drive a car. We do need to know how to start the car (which if you haven't bought a car lately, isn't as easy as it used to be). We need to know how to put the car in gear, and how to turn the wheel. We need to know when gas is needed, when to rotate the tires, and when to change the oil. Simple stuff, but it is required.

A well-designed financial strategy answers questions like:

1. How much can I spend during retirement without a strong chance of going broke?

2. What rate of return do I really need on my money, and how can I get it with the least amount of volatility?

3. How can I protect myself from speculation (stock picking, market timing)?

4. How will I deal with catastrophe, such as failing health?

5. How can I legally pay the IRS less?

6. How can I most efficiently transfer my assets at death?

Step Two: Creation

The questions in step one are answered by making you a participant in the plan's design. A good coach listens to what you want to accomplish (I want $X a month for life, after tax, indexed for inflation) and then offers the pros and cons behind the strategy toward achieving that goal. And believe us...there are always cons. Lots of them. You need to know them.

Together we will draw up your plan. How much of your income do you want guaranteed? Before you say, "all of it," know that guaranteed usually comes with two costs: low return and less for your heirs.

If you choose to have some or all your money in a non-guaranteed portfolio, do you fully understand the likely range of returns? What your worst year is likely to be (statistically)? And when it happens (and it will), what will you do?

How much (if any) would you like to leave your children?

How do you wish to handle the cost of custodial care should you need it (and you probably will)?

If you choose to make no changes, what are your chances for success? Are you okay with that?

Step Three: Consideration

Only after the design is fully complete can the plan be written. Back when Dan's blood results showed he had too much sugar, he and his doctor together discussed the ups and downs of the strategy: costs, time, denial of certain foods, etc. Once that was outlined, they created a written plan.

Medications can be used to fight illness. The doctor doesn't care where you fill the prescription. He simply wants you to fully take the meds.

In personal finance, products are the medication. While a coach can assist you in acquiring them, it should not be a requirement for being coached. Sadly, we too often see financial advisors offer "free" planning. There is no such thing as free. You will pay for it, one way or another. Typically, the "plan" is nothing more than a sales proposal to buy product. "We'll give you a free plan that will recommend you buy a commission-based product from us."

In addition to delivering the written plan, we provide the client with a list of recommendations on a single page. With each recommendation, we ask a few simple questions:

1. Do you fully understand this recommendation? Do you know the pros and cons?

2. Are you going to implement it (yes or no...never a "let me think about it")?

3. How are you going to implement it? Are you going work with someone (insurance agent, investment advisor)?

No loose ends.

Four: Coaching & Education Stage-

Our firm educates our clients in groups, but coaches them one on one. Some of the education classes reiterate important concepts that are helpful in understanding the long-term issues facing retirement. Other classes delve deeper into the client's emotions. Almost all our decisions are emotion based. We need to accept and understand that. By being in tune with our values, we are much more likely to reach a purpose for our money that reflects these values.

Our Offer to You

We would love for you to call our office and schedule a time for us to visit. You know our process and what to expect so there should be no surprises. Our office number is 770-382-5792 or visit our website at www.blackoakam.com.

About the Authors

Ryan is originally from Lilburn, Georgia in Gwinnett County and currently resides in Cumming, Georgia. He graduated from Parkview High School where he was drafted by the Tampa Bay Rays organization. Ryan played three years for the Tampa Bay Rays organization as well as the Pittsburgh Pirates organization for three years.

After a six-year professional baseball career, Ryan attended and graduated from the University of Georgia where he received his degree in Social Science Education. He then coached baseball and taught Economics at Brookwood High School in Snellville, Georgia for eight years. Ryan also has a master's degree from the University of Alabama and a Specialists degree from Lincoln Memorial University.

Ryan decided on a career change and entered the financial services industry in 2012. He joined Black Oak in September of 2013. Ryan takes his life experiences as a former professional baseball player and educator/coach and applies it to his practical approach in serving and building relationships with his clients. Ryan loves the personal approach that Black Oak takes with each and every client they serve. Ryan assists all age groups with their investments and retirement planning. Ryan loves being an educator and coach to his clients.

Ryan is married to Dr. Stephanie Ledden DVM who practices small animal medicine. She created her own business as a relief vet where she can work when and where she wants. They have two children (Lindy Grace and Lucas Ryan). In his spare time, Ryan enjoys keeping up with Georgia football, Atlanta Braves, playing golf, volunteering at his church, and most of all, spending time with his family and friends.

Dan Cuprill is a financial advisor from Cincinnati, OH. He co-authors books with other financial advisors by using the sections from his own book, <u>Retirement Rescue:</u> <u>Seven Lessons to Save Your Retirement.</u>

Made in the USA
Columbia, SC
01 October 2018